DAYS OF YOUR LIFE

DAYS OF YOUR LIFE

MAC MILLER LYRIC EDITION

BY MARINA CARDENAS

Charleston, SC
www.PalmettoPublishing.com

Days of Your Life

First Edition

Paperback ISBN: 979-8-8229-0346-3
eBook ISBN: 979-8-8229-0347-0

Now it's your turn to tell your story. From the author of *Days of My Life: Mac Miller Lyric Edition*, You got to hear bits and pieces of the life of Author Marina Cardenas. This therapeutic fill-in-the-blank self-care book prompts you to write down days of your life to the tune of Mac Miller lyrics. Mac Miller has been through different phases of our lives. His music saved and carried people through life's emotional rollercoaster. One thing Mac Miller always taught us to always get up and enjoy the ride to the beautiful destination.

"BE YOU...YOU'LL BE FINE."

—Mac Miller

This is *Days of Your Life: Self-Care Mac Miller Lyric Edition.*

I would like to thank all the Mac Miller fans. Without you guys, these books wouldn't exist. Mac is gone, but through us he lives on. I want to thank his mother and his team. No copyright infringement is intended. All songs are by Mac Miller. Part of the proceeds go to the nonprofit organization To Write Love on Her Arms (TWLOHA).

TWLOHA helps people who struggle with depression, anxiety, and substance abuse. You're not alone. I believe all of us Mac Miller fans are family and must stick together. He may not be with us, but he will forever be in our hearts.

92 until infinity.

Thank you for your purchase.

Love always,

MARINA CARDENAS

Gloomy days feel like when the sun's out but there's clouds all day. When there's ice cream but it's melted. When there's love but no person to give it to. So let's think of a gloomy day you've had:

Don't you know sunshine don't feel right when you inside all day?
I wish it was nice out but it looked like rain
Gray skies and I'm driftin, not livin forever
They told me it only gets better

SONG: "COME BACK TO EARTH"
ALBUM: SWIMMING.

Now let's write one positive thing about that gloomy day:

Sometimes you feel alone. People say, “Oh, I’ll be here when you need me.” It’s not good enough…you still feel alone. So you wait until you either realize there’s one person who has always cherished you or someone will walk into your life just in time.

Don’t give up.

Tell me a time when you felt alone:

____

____

____

____

____

Now think of one person who has made you smile or just someone who made your day a little better:

____

____

____

____

____

“And all I ever needed was somebody with some reason who can keep me sane”

SONG: “HAND ME DOWNS”
ALBUM: CIRCLES

In life you meet all kinds of people, you fall in love, or you picture how that relationship should be. What happens when you've tried everything and you're questioning if you're just staying because you're comfortable? You only have one life and even being alone to heal is ok. Bad relationships are not worth it. It's time to leave and find what makes you happy even if it scares you to leave.

Who is the person you wish you could be with? Or who is someone that has made you unhappy?

____

____

____

Now write three good things that came out of it...or if you didn't leave, write three things about your goals if you were to leave.

1. ____________________________________
____
2. ____________________________________
____
3. ____________________________________
____

"We don't even speak the same language I guess people always going through changes"

SONG: "MISSED CALLS"
ALBUM: BLUE SLIDE PARK

So let's be real…Life sucks. Sometimes we have problems, and it feels like every time we get a break—boom! Over and over we experience pain, tears, and disappointment. Despite everything, at the end of the day, life is a gift. We just need to have a positive attitude. We must change even if we have to start over.

When was a time you felt like nothing was going right:

___

___

___

___

___

How did you get back up? Or how will you?

___

___

___

___

___

"Now every day I wake up and breathe I don't have it all but that's alright with me…I struck out and came back swingin"

SONG: "2009"
ALBUM: SWIMMING

We don't give ourselves enough credit. We stop pursuing our dreams because the climb will take too long or they seem impossible to achieve. We have the power to achieve them, but the question is: when will you start working on those goals? How hard are you willing to go? When will you will say, "Today is the day!"

My dream is:

____

____

____

____

____

The first step I will take is:

____

____

____

____

____

"Somehow we got to find a way No matter how many miles it takes Put the ladder all the way until we touching the sky."

SONG: "LADDERS"
ALBUM: SWIMMING

Habits are scary. They can either be good or bad. They're all we know. It becomes normal or is it normal? Bad habits might feel normal until you realize they just end up hurting you. One must experience the good habit to get rid of the bad ones.

What are three bad habits you have?

____

____

____

Now three good habits:

____

____

____

How can we get rid of the bad ones? Let's replace them with the three good ones:

____

____

____

*"I don't know how the normal shit go, so I guess I'll just play it by ear, Silence is all that I hear.
Listening close as I can growing up (one, two, three) jump nobody holding my hand tho"*

SONG: "WINGS"
ALBUM: SWIMMING

What's the point in having a best friend who judges you, someone who is only there when it's convenient? Not everyone is your friend. Your friend should listen to and support you. If you're sad about the same thing, talk about it one thousand times. Your REAL friend would listen 1,000 times because they are your true friend. Real friends listen, care, and don't make you feel like a burden. Make sure any friendship or relationship is fifty/fifty.

Has a "friend" ever made you feel judged?

Write down what a real friend is to you:

"Yeah I'm only keeping good company I'm not talking to you if you don't have love for me"

SONG: "PROGRAMS"

Don't feel bad when you're not someone's type. Everyone is made differently, and that's beautiful. So what if you're not their type? That just means it's not worth sharing your unique qualities with them. Don't waste the beauty of your heart on a broken mirror.

What's one reason someone said they couldn't be with you or didn't like you?

____

____

____

____

Now let's name some amazing things about you or a compliment someone said about you:

____

____

____

____

"I've never seen somebody put together perfectly... someone like you is so hard to find"

SONG: "OBJECTS IN THE MIRROR"
ALBUM: WATCHING MOVIES WITH THE SOUND OFF

Certain people come into our lives to teach us a self-care lesson. Be careful because caring about what others think and trying to please people will drain you. We often put our time and effort into others, but we need to be our number-one priority. Some people will make you feel guilty when you choose yourself. We need to make sure you don't get stuck in being a people pleaser.

Now let's think about you. Write down different ways to say "no" but kindly, so that hard situations can become easier to refuse.

- ______________________________
  ____
- ______________________________
  ____
- ______________________________
  ____
- ______________________________
  ____
- ______________________________
  ____

"Why can't it be easy, why does everybody need me to stay?...All I do is say sorry Half the time I don't even know what I'm saying it about...No more, no more, no more."

SONG: "GOOD NEWS"
ALBUMS: CIRCLES

We often find ourselves stressed. We feel as if we need to figure out one problem after another. Next thing you know we have tons of problems. What are three of yours?

1. ______________________________

____

2. ______________________________

____

3. ______________________________

____

Mac Miller said in this song:

He looked up and smiled, asked me, "How do you do?"
I told him, "I'm losing my grip"
He told me, "Son, if you want to hold on to yourself.
Then let yourself slip."

To me, I believe he was saying if you hold on to every problem—every situation that causes you stress, anger, anxiety, depression—it will weigh you down. We're so afraid to hit rock bottom, but if you just let go, tackle everything head on, and accept what you can't change, you won't know how strong you are. Without falling you won't grow into who you really need to be. The only way is up when you fall and hit the bottom. Remember there's always a bottom.

SONG: "COLORS AND SHAPES"
ALBUM: FACES

What's one thing you never thought you could get over, perhaps an obstacle, a heartbreak, or a situation? You're here! Time to swim up, not straight.

I made it through:

I'm here because:

I'm stronger now because:

My anxiety used to be so bad. I would cancel plans, stay in mostly, avoid big crowds. My mind would stack issues that weren't even there. It once got so bad I avoided any contact. The minimum. I realized I started missing out. Not on life but on me. I was a beautiful, fun,social butterfly. How did I become so afraid of the world that I would keep myself locked away when I had the key? One day I got the opportunity to go to Pittsburgh all inclusive. Blue slide park, come on! It took me a month of therapy to finally get on that plane. That's how bad my anxiety was. Point of this story was that I got on that plane and had an amazing trip. It was a struggle no one knew about. It was a month of hard work to get out there. I was proud of myself. It was progress. No matter how small your victory, celebrate it. Give yourself credit.

Tell about small victory, accomplishment, or creation you made, anything you're proud of:

"So many things that I've created but this right here might be my favorite They ask me how I feel I say, 'Amazing I feel amazing"

SONG: "HERE WE GO"
ALBUM: FACES

Depression can be really hard. We don't choose to be depressed. The brain is a complicated part of our bodies. Mac said in the song "San Francisco," "Welcome to the dark side of my bizarre mind, / I'm trapped inside of this amusement park ride." That's what depression feels like to me, a bad, crazy roller coaster ride you can't get off of, and when you think you can get off, the ride starts again. One day you'll realize that roller coaster is made by your brain, but you are the engineer so you can change it to a smooth ride. You must learn to control your thoughts. Don't let them control you. It's your theme park.

Draw a picture of your new brain roller coaster ride. Get creative! Create happy characters, scenery, and positivity only. "New Ride Opening Soon!"

Enter roller coaster name here:

(____)

Use the rest of the page as the layout:

This section is dedicated to my best friend:

ORLANDO A. FUENTES
OCT. 14, 1992—MAR. 8, 2022

Orlando Fuentes was my best friend since middle school. We were always together. He was my sweet, little Lando. I sat by myself. I was new to school with no friends. He saw me and said, "Hey, why are you sitting alone? I'm just going to sit with you so people don't laugh at you." We both smiled as he sat down. We talked and laughed so much. From that day I knew he was special. We became best friends, inseparable. You know when you meet someone who just gets it? We would hang out every day after school, play basketball, and just laugh. It was a beautiful friendship. Nothing and no one could break us apart. I was never judged, never let down. Lando was there through the heartbreak and struggles. If it had to do with me, he would be there in a heartbeat no questions asked.

Although we were best friends, I knew he was madly in love with me. I was the queen of his kingdom. When I was getting let down and hurt by others, he knew I deserved more. He didn't have to tell me because I knew, I always knew. You know the movies where the guy loves the girl, but they're just best friends? The thing about Lando was he would rather be best friends and spend every day with me than not have me. Very respectful, he valued our friendship. He was very kind, loving, and was the only person who knew my heart. He knew me.

Fast forward to adulthood. On Oct 20th, 2021: At 10:50 p.m. he texted me saying he was sick and asked for me not to cry or be worried. He would be fine. I finally got it out of him. He told me he had Stage 4 stomach cancer. My heart dropped, shattered, busted. I went numb. I called him, crying, yet he still had strength to comfort me. He said, "You know, Marina, I never want to hurt you or make you cry. I'll lose my perfect record." We laughed because I couldn't believe how he wanted to keep his perfect record.

The nights were our time to text all night up to 4:00 a.m. just talking about life. It wasn't until he got worse that the calls stopped, the texts shrank in length. He was so tired with the cancer was talking over his body. It hurt me because he kept telling me, "I want to go home. I can see you if I can just go home. I'm tired." Yet with the tiny bit of strength he had he would text me, "I'm ok. Just tired. Need rest." I said, "My little Lando, you will make it and will travel the world just like you always wanted to. Just fight...I love you." I knew in my heart my sweet Lando was going to the most beautiful place, and I was losing him. In every text he was so strong, so unselfish. One thing about Lando was when he would let you in his heart, if he loved you or chose to keep you in his life, he always showed nothing but pure love. It wasn't until he wrote to me, "I'll never regret making you my best friend. I wasn't popular in school, but I want to let you know when you and I were together nothing else mattered." That's when my worth hit me. He saw me, my worth.

He showed me how love is supposed to be. He was my best friend, but this whole time he showed me how special I was. He was honored to be my best friend, which was crazy to me because I was really the one who felt honored. God created a person so beautiful not one bit of selfishness or hate lived in his heart. My eyes opened up, and I will not have anyone in my life who doesn't treat me any less than my sweet Lando. This was his lesson to me. When he was running out of time, he spoke the words of his heart so I could finally know how much I meant to him. We didn't have enough time because God needed his angel back. In tears I told my best friend, "You are strong, a fighter, for not once did you give up. Thank you for loving me and for the memories. I wouldn't have been able to go through life without you." He said me too, "I love you so much, Marina. I'll always be here." I cried, "Don't forget about me." He said, "I never do." I said, "k love you good night." That was the last text, and he was gone. My sweet Lando, I'm sorry you were in pain.

I would be selfish if I wanted you to stay with pain of cancer every day. You finally can rest. You're home now. At his funeral they asked if anyone wanted to speak. I didn't want to share my poem, but my heart felt a jump. It wouldn't stop, and I knew it was Lando telling me to get up and share it. So here it goes:

In honor of my best friend who fought until his last breath:

My Sweet Lando

My sweet Lando you were my best friend when hearts were broken you were there to mend. We didn't care what anyone would say. You were always my sun when my skies were gray.

You said it was you and I

Never did I think this day would happen where I'd have to say goodbye

My sweet Lando with the beautiful colored eyes showed the beautiful person who was inside my protector, my best friend, my ride or die.

I feel your soul every time I cry you let me know that you're still alive I can't bring you back no matter how much I pray.

But I understand god needed his angel as much as I wanted you to stay.

You said "Be strong"

I'm trying my best but I'm barely holding on.

One day I'll see you again.

Forever and always my sweet friend.

The last word you said to me was just know you're in my heart and I will always hold on to that part.

Now you're an angel in heaven up above.

Thank you for taking care of all the people you loved.

Rest in peace my little Lando

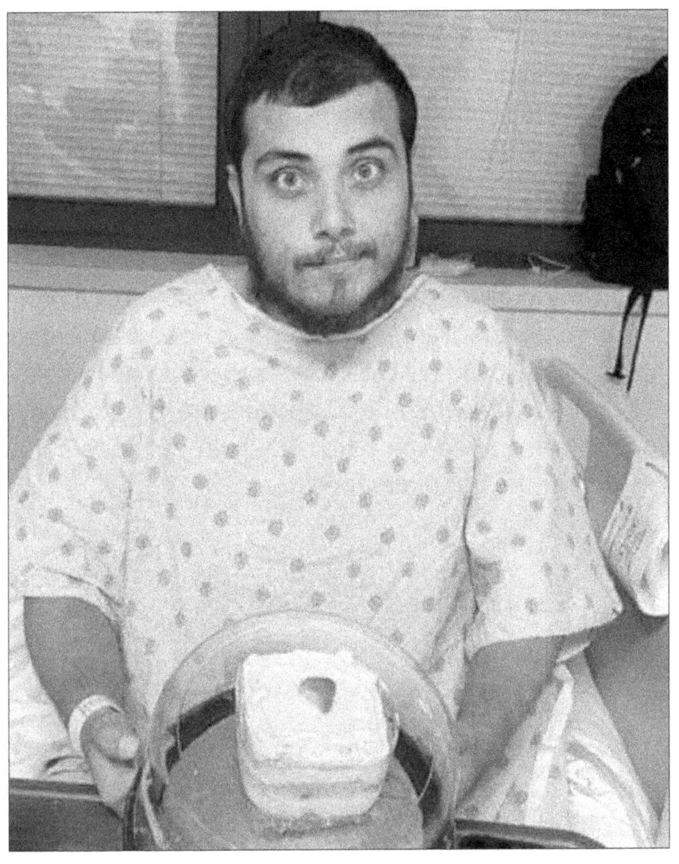

"If you hear what heaven is like can you tell me?...See everybody you want"

SONG: "THE SCOOP ON HEAVEN"
ALBUM: I LOVE LIFE, THANK YOU

I remember when I was a kid when someone passed away I didn't understand. I remember going to my grandpa's funeral and seeing tears, pain, and sadness, but I was just kind of there. Once I got older, I realized death comes with heartbreak. It's sadly part of life because none of us are forever. But this isn't a sad book. Our good memories are more important. When my Lando died, I remember us at school, laughing and enjoying good times. Our laughs put a smile on my face. When my aunt passed away, and I remember before she died all she wanted was a pound of sweet bread. My uncle he loved his cigarettes and would always say, "I'll rest enough when I die" because we would always tell him he worked too hard. The pain will ease if you remember the good memories.

Let's pay some of our loved ones respect and write an enjoyable memory of what made them so special.

Let's start with our one and only:

1. Rip Dates

Name: Malcom Mccormick 1992–2018

Memory:

____

____

____

____

____

____

2. Rip Dates

Name:

Memory:

____

____

____

____

____

____

3. Rip Dates

Name:

Memory:

____

____

____

____

____

____

"It's a blue world without you"

"Well if you can see me now loving and holding it down"

SONG: "BLUE WORLD"
ALBUM: CIRCLES

When you're a kid, you don't care what anyone thinks, but as we get older we become more aware. Do you ever think, "Man, I wish I was a kid. That was when I was brave and didn't care. That was when I was really me"? Let's name three things you remember as a kid good positive traits you had

1. ______________________________

____

2. ______________________________

____

3. ______________________________

____

Now let's write what you miss and how you can get back to some things to bring that happy kid out:

____

____

____

____

____

____

____

"I've always been the same kid…It's better to be yourself, don't ever just live a lie."

SONG: "I LOVE LIFE, THANK YOU"
ALBUM: I LOVE LIFE, THANK YOU

Sometimes I feel rushed. I learned in life you're not supposed to go at another person's pace. It's your life, your time. It will happen...slow down, take your time.

Name three things you feel you are rushing through in life:

1. ______________________________

____

2. ______________________________

____

3. ______________________________

____

Now let's write a plan. Let's slow it down.

If it didn't work out, why didn't it?

____

____

____

____

____

"Everybody keep rushing Why aren't we taking our time?...Don't keep it all in your head...I think you getting it now."

SONG: "ONCE A DAY"
ALBUM: CIRCLES

If someone gave you a chance to relive a moment, where would you go? Would you go to a time when you were happy or a time when you were sad? Happy, right? But the irony is when you come back to the happy moment you chose you will become sad in your future. If you choose the sad moment, you would see how strong you have become and how far you've made it.

Have you ever been judged or like people think they know you? Sometimes people make this whole different picture on who you are. We start to lose ourselves when you care what people say. I learned that once you realize who you are and let go of people who mistake your character you will be able to be your full self. No opinions, no accusations. Be you, and don't let anyone put in your head that anything is wrong with you. This attitude can make you happier.

What's your favorite thing about yourself? Own it:

____

____

____

____

____

____

____

____

"When you always be the subject of discussion But it's nothing when you stop and just say "Fuck It"

"And mother fuckers think they know me but they never met the kid"

SONG: "DONALD TRUMP"
ALBUM: BEST DAY EVER

I need you to make that change. If you fall, get back up. Something didn't work? Try something different. Scared do it? Life sucks? Change things. I need you to try, try, and try again, and when you're sick and tired on the floor crying, I need you to get the fuck up! No help? Do things yourself, but one thing you can't do is give up. You're still here for a reason. Your time is coming. It might take awhile for things to get better, but it won't happen if you don't keep trying.

Let me see you write how you have survived and kept going in the past:

____

____

____

____

____

____

____

____

____

____

"I'm just doing what I gotta...Weight I'm carrying, gotta let it go It won't hold me down no more"

SONG: "100 GRANDKIDS"
ALBUM: GO:OD AM

Anger...let's talk about it. What makes you angry?

- ____
- ____
- ____
- ____
- ____

Now let's think about that. Does anger do anything but harm your peace? Yes, right—holding on to anger causes you to destroy your growth. It's not worth it. You can't control what happens around or to you, but you can choose how you react to it on the inside. We need to let go of anger, be in the moment, then breathe, and let it go. Now breathe, hold it in, for five seconds...Now let go.

"Do as a Saint do, turn painful to graceful Devil on my trails I'm trying to find the holy grail"

SONG: "SUPLEXES INSIDE OF COMPLEXES AND DUPLEXES"
ALBUM: WATCHING MOVIES WITH THE SOUND OFF

It's ok to feel lost. Sometimes we think we have our life planned out, and then all the sudden it's not what we thought. Being lost along your journey is a chance for you to enjoy the moment. You can lose your way, but make sure you find the destination when it feels right. You might be alone, and that's ok. You might have started with support and lost some on the way. That's ok too. Just arrive.

Where do you want to arrive?

"Peace don't seem possible when the mind is so closed still searching for something but I don't know what"

SONG: "SOMEONE LIKE YOU"
ALBUM: WATCHING MOVIES WITH THE SOUND OFF

Disappointment is one of the worst experiences, especially when it's back to back to back. I know people say, "Think positive." To me I feel like if I put everyone and everything on a step stool and expect them to love, care, and be like me to be exactly how it's made in my head makes things worse when I'm disappointed. We are better off if we don't expect anything and just witness the results of our actions.

The less you expect, the less disappointment will hurt, and when someone or something exceeds our expectations the happiness is worth it.

Let's name some high expectations or some disappointments you've had:

In summary, let's write what we learned and how we can move forward from not hurting ourselves.

"ya'll can't tell me nothing no more Came from the basement under that floor."

"All I wanna do is the most...I was out of town gettin' lost till I was rescued now I'm in the clouds."

SONG: "JET FUEL"
ALBUM: SWIMMING

One day I was working and someone told me, "How are you so bubbly and happy all the time? We love your personality. It's like sunshine." I told her, "Really?" She replied, "That, or you're amazing at hiding that you're miserable." She laughed, and so did I. While I laughed, inside I was crying because I was depressed, dead inside. I couldn't understand how the happy, bubbly me couldn't be on the inside.

Why was it so impossible? That's when it hit me: my goal was to make that person on the outside exist on the inside, and I wouldn't stop until I achieved that.

Do you feel like that sometimes?

Why?

Now let's really figure out what is causing that lack of inner positivity. What can we do to make us feel better on the inside? Let's change, because we're worth it, right? Talk to me. Let's do it!

"And she asked me "why the long face?"...Today is full of regret, find forever into tomorrow...I know it seems a little bit strange sometimes"

"That's life...And I'm headed to the other side where the grass is always greener."

SONG: "THAT'S LIFE"

One day you will look back and see that the pain, the suffering, the depression, and the dark times will have worthwhile meaning. I believe in you. I may not know you, but if you're like me, I got issues that I'm still working on, and I'm learning what brings me love, peace, and happiness. I've been through so much and so have you. I believe in you even if no one else does. I know you can do it. It's hard, but do it for yourself. Mac always said:

"No matter where life takes me, find me with a smile. Pursuit to be happy only laughing like a child. I never thought life would be this sweet."

What Mac song gets you through your day?

____

____

____

____

SONG: "BDE"
ALBUM: BEST DAY EVER

Answer these questions for me: How are you going to get up? How are we going to fight and make ourselves better when we feel depression, anxiety, suicide, or just any negative thought? Remember you are special. Love yourself. Remember the real, happy you.

"Life goes on days get brighter...In a world that go round Are you up or down? You in, or you out? You smile, or you frown? Just get up! Get up!"

SONG: "GET UP"
ALBUM: BDE

You give yourself away when you love people who are toxic. You give time and waste years on people who take the life out of you. Have you ever been in a dark place where it seems impossible to climb out of? Do you ever feel drained? Do you experience anxiety, depression, suicide?

Now let's breathe, and tell me what's got you drained:

____

____

____

____

____

____

____

____

____

You are worthy. Your life will get better, even if it seems impossible. Mac always told us not to give up and to keep going. We're too busy pleasing people that we forget about ourselves.

You've wasted years on people, situations, anxiety, depression, and negativity. Now it's time to spend years on you. Write down what makes you happy. No one else—JUST YOU. I want you to try your hardest to follow your happy list. We all have a story. You decide what life you want.

If you're living a life that you don't you can change it , what makes you happy?

Read this every day to remind yourself, "I have one life and it's mine!"

Release yourself. It's time to be happy to be free. Be positive and remember that self-care comes first. I believe in you, and Mac Miller believes in you. He gave us the best gift—his music. His spirit will forever be with us. Let's say these words that he left us with together:

"Self care I'm treating me right / Hell yea we gonna be alright / … / Self care we gonna be good."

SONG: "SELF CARE"
ALBUM: SWIMMING

ALWAYS REMEMBER THE
BEST DAY EVER

92 TILL INFINITY.

www.ingramcontent.com/pod-product-compliance
Ingram Content Group UK Ltd.
Pitfield, Milton Keynes, MK11 3LW, UK
UKHW021934190726
13853UKWH00004B/1431

9 798822 903463